HOW TO CARE FOR YOUR NEW PET

CARING FOR
MY NEW
PUPPY

John Bankston

Mitchell Lane

PUBLISHERS

2001 SW 31st Avenue
Hallandale, FL 33009
www.mitchelllane.com

First Edition, 2019.

Author: John Bankston
Designer: Ed Morgan
Editor: Sharon F. Doorasamy

Names/credits:
Title: Caring for My New Puppy / by John Bankston
Description: Hallandale, FL : Mitchell Lane Publishers, [2019]

Series: How to Care for Your New Pet

Library bound ISBN: 9781680203226

eBook ISBN: 9781680203233

Photo credits: Design elements and photos, Freepik.com, p. 8-9 Olivia Spink on Unsplash, p. 10-11 Marcus Wallis on Unsplash, p. 12-13 Olivia Spink on Unsplash, p. 16-17 Hyunwon Jang on Unsplash, p. 22-23 James Barker on Unsplash, p. 24-25 Matthew Henry on Unsplash

CONTENTS

Words in **bold** throughout can be found in the Glossary.

A Brief History of Dogs

You might choose a Chihuahua. You might get a German Shepard. Every dog is related to the wolf. Thousands of years ago, wolves followed people. People littered. Wolves ate the food they left behind.

The wolves kept getting closer. Successful wolves were brave and gentle. They got the most food from people. They had more puppies. People started living with wolves. They started hunting together.

Dogs still help people. They find missing children. They assist the disabled. They work for police and firefighters. The first animal to be tamed is one of the most popular pets. No matter what type of dog, it is friendly and loyal.

Dog Facts

Few animals have more variety than dogs. The smallest Chihuahua weighs a few pounds. The biggest Saint Bernard can weigh more than 200 pounds. Dogs have been bred to act a certain way. Adult dogs behave like wolf puppies. They are curious and love to play.

Dogs have an amazing sense of smell. It is at least 10,000 times better than ours. They also have better hearing.

Purebred dogs have parents that are the same breed. Their grandparents and great-grandparents were also the same breed—all the way to the breed's beginnings. There are nearly 400 different purebred dogs.

Most dogs have parents that are different breeds. "Mutts" or mixed-breed dogs are often healthier. There are also "designer" dogs. These are mixed-breed dogs whose parents were selected. The Labradoodle is a Labrador retriever and a poodle. A beagle and a pug were bred to produce a puggle. A ChiJack is a Chihuahua and a Jack Russell terrier.

Every breed has different qualities. If you like a certain breed, learn as much as you can about it before getting one.

Puppy Planning

Start with a family meeting. You won't need much help caring for a goldfish or a gerbil. Puppies are different. Everyone in your house will be involved. You will want to teach younger brothers and sisters how to safely play with the puppy. If you leave for school, an adult might walk or feed it. Puppies shouldn't be alone for too long.

You can discuss breeds. Different dogs have different needs. Golden retrievers are famously friendly. They also need space to run.

Chihuahuas thrive in small places. But they can be shy or hard to **socialize**.

You will feed and walk your puppy the most. You should be the one who trains it. Others will pitch in. It's a good idea to talk about who will do what. Everyone has to learn the same commands. If you say "stay" and someone else says "down," for the same thing, then the puppy will be confused.

You might decide not to get a puppy. Puppies are cute and frisky. They can also wake you up because they are scared. They have accidents. They chew shoes.

Adult dogs are often housebroken. They are usually better being alone. They can love and lick you as much as a puppy. Most puppy tips work with any new dog.

Puppy Proofed

Before you pick out a puppy, pick out where it will stay. Puppies can get in a lot of trouble. They need a clean, safe space. A spare bathroom works well. So does the corner of a kitchen or your room. You may need a gate or puppy pen. Don't let a puppy roam around your house.

Outside **kennels** can get too hot or too cold. Basements and garages are also bad for puppies. Puppies try to eat lots of things. Paint, antifreeze, and detergent are **poisonous** to dogs.

After selecting a place, get on your hands and knees. Now you have a puppy eye view. Remove things like plants or trash bins. Have an adult help you cover unused outlets. Plastic tubes can be put over electrical cords. Puppies sometimes chew those. Latch any cabinets or drawers that a puppy can open.

DID YOU KNOW?

To help people with disabilities, canine companions train eight hours a day for six to nine months.

DID YOU KNOW?

The American Kennel Society lists seven types of purebred dogs: sporting dogs, hounds, working dogs, terriers, toy dogs, nonsporting dogs, and herding dogs.

Puppy Prep

Bringing home a new dog is exciting. It's also a little scary. Make your life and your puppy's life easier. Get a few things first.

A dog bed made for puppies can help. Or you may want to get a crate. These plastic or metal **carriers** offer a safe space for a puppy. When you bring a puppy home, it may have a towel or blanket that it sleeps with. Put it in the bed or crate. This will help it sleep better.

If you have a puppy pen, set it up.

Your dog will need two small metal bowls. Metal is easier to keep clean than ceramic. Dogs can chew plastic bowls. If they swallow a piece it can be bad for them. Set the bowls near the crate or inside the pen.

A chew toy or two will be a good gift when a puppy comes home. Buy ones that are made for puppies.

You should also get a leash. A **harness** is best for puppies and small dogs. Unlike a collar, it lets you pull the puppy up quickly without hurting it.

Because your puppy will be used to eating a certain kind of dog food, you should wait to buy this.

Puppy Picking

If you already know the kind of dog you want, visit a breeder. Breeders raise specific breeds, such as German Shepards or beagles. If a friend has the breed of dog you like, find out where they got it.

Are you open to different breeds? Maybe you just want a small dog or a dog that likes to fetch. Consider **adopting**. Every day, thousands of dogs are left at shelters and rescue centers. Most are friendly and healthy. They just had owners who couldn't take care of them. Shelter dogs are so happy to find a forever home. It might take time to **bond**. But a mixed-breed dog is usually healthier than a purebred.

Sites for shelters or rescue centers show available dogs. Have an adult help you look. There are so many to choose from! You can also go to a "Pet Rescue Day." These events have booths where you can meet all kinds of dogs and puppies.

If a dog belonging to someone you know has puppies, this can be a great way to **adopt**. Knowing what the mother is like can help you see how her puppies will behave. Your new friend needs to stay with its mom for at least two months.

If you adopt a dog from a stranger, you won't know the dog's health history. You could be bringing home a sick or mistreated dog.

Homecoming

Spend time with the puppy before it comes home. At the breeder, try to meet its mother. Take a look at the puppy's eyes. Are they bright? Does it have a shiny coat? The puppy should have a lot of energy. If it hides in a corner or tries to avoid you, it may be sick.

Shelters will also let you spend time with the puppy. Sometimes the mother will be there too. Find out as much as you can about the puppy. Play with it.

Usually you have to wait to take the puppy home. This gives you time to think. Are you sure you want to take care of it? Are you ready to walk it, feed it, deal with accidents? It's okay if you don't feel ready. It's better to not get a puppy than to get one you can't handle.

If you do get the puppy, the shelter or breeder will tell you the puppy chow it has been eating. You will want to give it the same food. You can change it later. Right now, moving to a brand new home is change enough.

Bringing your puppy home is an exciting day. It's like school vacation and your birthday combined. It's pretty exciting for your puppy too. It's leaving its home to go to a brand new one. The puppy probably will be nervous. It may have an accident. Don't get mad. The puppy just has to get used to you and its new family.

You should have a crate or carrier for your puppy. This will make the trip easier. The shelter or breeder may give you a towel from its bed. Place it inside the carrier. Secure the carrier with a seatbelt.

Holding a dog on your lap in a moving car is a bad idea. The dog can escape. It can distract the driver or jump from a window. It can get hurt.

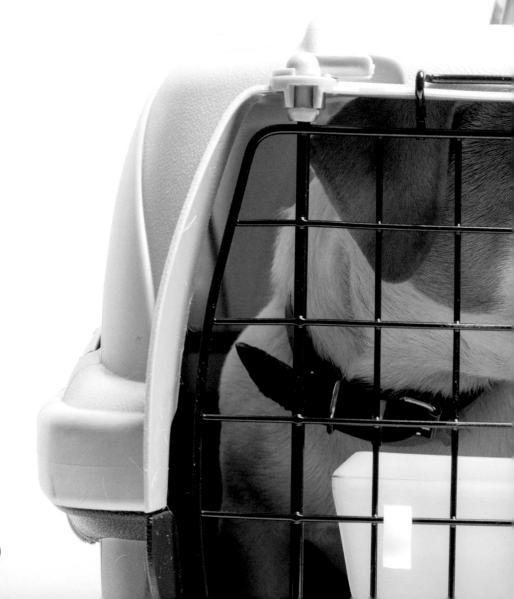

If you have a younger brother or sister, they probably sit in a car seat. They aren't left alone when everyone else goes inside. Try to treat your puppy like a baby. Make sure they are secure in the car. Don't leave them alone.

When you get home give your puppy a walk. If it goes to the bathroom, tell the puppy how good it is.

DID YOU KNOW?

A puppy can hold its urine for one hour for every month of age. A three-month old puppy can hold it for three hours. Adult dogs should be walked every six-to-eight hours.

House Breaking

Training your puppy is hard. Puppies don't have a lot of control. They are just learning.

Walking your dog is very important. It gets it used to going outside at a certain time. The puppy should be walked right after you wake up and just before you go to sleep. It should also be walked once or twice in the middle of the day. The best time is after a nap.

Most puppies can't hold their **urine** all night. Leave newspapers near its bed or crate. Dogs don't like to soil their den. Its crate is its den. Inside the crate you should put a chew toy, a blanket, and fresh water. Make sure the crate isn't too big. If it is, your puppy will use one corner as a potty. Keeping it in the crate at night reduces accidents.

Be happy and friendly when the puppy poops outside. You might catch it trying to poop in the house. Say, "No," in a firm voice. Pick it up. Puppies usually stop going if you pick them up. Carry it outside. Set the puppy down and tell it how good it is when it goes. Never hit or yell at your puppy. Yelling won't train it. It will only teach your puppy to be scared of you.

Food and Water

The right food for your puppy is very important. Growing from a puppy to a dog in a year takes energy. That's why puppies sleep so much. It's also why they should be fed three to four times a day. How much and how often depends on the **breed**.

Adult dogs like to be fed twice a day. Just make sure it's only half their food for each meal.

Dogs like meat and vegetables. Good dog foods should have both. They should have more meat than grain.

Dog food used to be whatever people didn't eat. Today, many pet food companies raise cows, ducks, chickens, and other animals just for dog food. Farms grow fruits and vegetables just for dogs too.

Healthy food helps make a healthy pup.

Keep water in one of its bowls. Rinse it out and add fresh water at least once a day. Don't let it get empty. However, if they don't eat or stop eating they may be sick. This is why going to a **veterinarian** is so important.

DO NOT FEED YOUR DOG:

Chocolate (especially dark chocolate), macadamia nuts, onions, grapes, or raisins. These foods can make your dog very sick. If it eats one of these foods, tell an adult right away. Sugar free candy and gum have **xylitol** which is dangerous for dogs.

Visiting the Vet

Soon after you bring your puppy home, you will want to bring it to a veterinarian. This is a special doctor that only treats animals. Often rescue centers have their own veterinarians. If you adopted your puppy at a shelter or purchased it from a breeder, they will know a good vet. Friends with dogs can also help.

The vet will check your puppy's heart, look in its ears, and give it a check up. He or she can tell you what shots your puppy will need. The vet will also be able to give you tips about caring for your pup.

Before your puppy is an adult, you will want to have it **neutered**. This is between six months to a year. It depends on the breed. Getting your dog neutered will keep it from making puppies. It's hard finding good homes for all the puppies born every day. Your puppy was lucky. It has found its forever home.

Tricks for Treats

You start training your puppy right away. You might not know it. It acts a certain way because of how you act. Maybe it starts whining in its crate. You rush over and pick it up. Now you've trained your puppy. It knows that when its whines, you will take care of it. The more your puppy whines, the more attention it gets.

This is probably not what you want. Instead, wait until it's quiet. This can take a while. But when it's finally quiet, say "Good girl or boy," and give it a small treat.

Your puppy will spend more time with your hands than any other part of you. Teach it that your hands are kind. They pet. They give treats. You can even hand-feed your puppy. As it gets used to your hands, you will be able to lightly touch its paws. You will be able to brush its fur. You will even be able to brush its teeth. This is very important. Always use a toothpaste for dogs. Don't use people paste!

All dogs are different. Even two Chihuahuas or two beagles aren't exactly alike. Some dogs are high-energy. Others are shy. High-energy dogs are outgoing. They love meeting people or other dogs. They can also be hard to train. They always want to do new things.

A shy dog might do fine in your house. They forget their training when you go for a walk. Puppies need kindness and a sweet voice.

If you have a dog that barks or snaps at you, you may need to work with a trainer.

Most puppies are happy to learn. Pick a time right before feeding. Give it a treat when it does well. Before long, your puppy will be a well-trained dog.

DID YOU KNOW?

Neutered dogs are less likely to stray or try to get out of your yard.

SHOPPING LIST

When you are ready to bring home a puppy or a dog, have an adult take you to your local pet store. This is a list of some things you will need:

- ☐ Crate
- ☐ Gate
- ☐ Dog bed with warm blanket or towel
- ☐ Two metal bowls
- ☐ Chew toys
- ☐ Premium puppy food
- ☐ Safety dog collar with ID tag or harness
- ☐ Leash or lead
- ☐ Brush
- ☐ Wipes
- ☐ Toys, grooming supplies, bedding, collar, and odor neutralizer

FIND OUT MORE

Online

There are a number of sites to learn about cat rescue centers in your area:

Humane Society:
   http://m.humanesociety.org

Petfinder:
   https://www.petfinder.com/animal-shelters-and-rescues/search/

Several national pet supply chains have also partnered with rescue organizations. There are also "pet rescue days" held at fairs and swap meets.

Paws will help you get more involved with helping animals. They can also connect you with shelters:
   https://www.paws.org/kids

The American Kennel Club has information on purebred dogs and dog shows:
   https://www.apps.akc.org/apps/kids_juniors/index.cfm?nav_area=kids_juniorsPet names: Here's a fun site to find a great pet name

   https://www.bowwow.com.au

Here are some more tips for when you bring your new friend home:
   https://www.petfinder.com/dogs/bringing-a-dog-home/preparing-home-new-dog/

   https://pets.webmd.com/dogs/guide/puppy-care

   http://www.vetstreet.com/new-dog-owner-guide

Before you take your new best friend to the dog park, this video shows different ways dogs behave.
   https://www.petfinder.com/videos/dog-parks-and-aggression-in-dogs-with-other-dogs/

Woof: It's a Dog's Life host Matthew Margolis offers advice on dog training:
   http://www.pbs.org/wgbh/woof/tips/index.html

Books

Pelar, Colleen, and Amber Johnson. *Puppy Training for Kids*. Hauppauge, NY: Barron's Educational, 2012.

Presnall, Judith Janda. *Canine Companions*. San Diego, CA: Kidhaven Press, 2016.

Skiles, Janet. *How to Care for Your Dog: A Color & Learn Guide for Kids*. Dover Publications, 2011.

GLOSSARY

adopt/adopting
Choosing or taking something as your own

bond
Joining together

breeds
A particular type or kind of animal

carrier
Safe container to transport an animal

harness
Straps and fabric used to control an animal

kennels
Small shelter for a dog

neutered
To have part of the sex organs of an animal removed so that it cannot reproduce

poisonous
Substance that is dangerous or deadly

socialized
Comfortable playing and being around others

urine
Liquid waste excreted by people and animals

veterinarian
An animal doctor

xylitol
A naturally occurring alcohol found in plants which is used as a sweetener

BIBLIOGRAPHY

"Bringing Home a New Puppy." WebMD. https://pets.webmd.com/dogs/guide/bringing-home-new-puppy#1.

Becker, Dr. Marty, DVM. "Surviving Your First 30 Days With a New Puppy." *Vetstreet*, June 22, 2015. http://www.vetstreet.com/dr-marty-becker/surviving-your-first-30-days-with-a-new-puppy?page=2.

Flanagan, Jane K. "How to Talk to Your Dog." Petfinder. https://www.petfinder.com/dogs/dog-training/talk-to-your-dog/.

"How to Housetrain your Dog or Puppy." The Humane Society. http://m.humanesociety.org/animals/dogs/tips/housetraining_puppies.html.

Lester, Toby. "The Slippery Slope to Extinction." *Wall Street Journal*, March 20, 2015. https://www.wsj.com/articles/book-review-the-invaders-by-pat-shipman-1426884980.

Margolis, Matthew. " The Right Way to Train a Dog." *Woof: It's a Dog's Life.* http://www.pbs.org/wgbh/woof/tips/tip_01.html.

Presnall, Judith Janda. "Canine Companions: Training Dogs to Become Partners." *Canine Companions.* San Diego, CA: KidHaven Press, 2016.

Tyson, Peter. "Dogs' Dazzling Sense of Smell." NOVA Science NOW, October 4, 2012. http://www.pbs.org/wgbh/nova/nature/dogs-sense-of-smell.html.

INDEX

ABOUT THE AUTHOR

John Bankston

The author of over 100 books for young readers, John Bankston lives in Miami Beach, Florida, with his ChiJack rescue dog named Astronaut. He adopted Astronaut from the Alicia Pet Care Center in Mission Viejo, California. (https://www.mypetsdr.com).